THE SAME THINGS

Words and Music by Jamie Cullum
and Ben Cullum

JAMIE CULLUM   MOMENTUM

MUSIC ARRANGED BY TOM RICHARDS

ISBN 978-1-4803-5279-7

HAL•LEONARD®
CORPORATION
7777 W. BLUEMOUND RD. P.O. BOX 13819 MILWAUKEE, WI 53213

Visit Hal Leonard Online at
www.halleonard.com

TOM RICHARDS

Tom is a saxophonist, multi instrumentalist, composer and arranger and has been fortunate to work with some of the biggest names in music. Tom currently plays for Jamie Cullum, Gary Barlow and Tim Minchin as well as his own projects. He has been touring and recording with Jamie Cullum since 2005, and in 2010 was arranger and musical director for Jamie's prom at the Royal Albert Hall. Other arranging credits include Tim Minchin's orchestral arena tour and DVD with the Heritage Orchestra, Massive Attack's re-imagining of the Blade Runner soundtrack, UNKLE, Dizzee Rascal, The Streets and Basement Jaxx. Tom is also a house writer for the legendary Metropole Orchestra in Holland and is a trusted TV and film orchestrator. As a leader, Tom's 2006 release on Candid Records, *Smoke and Mirrors,* is a showcase for his own writing for his 20 piece Jazz Orchestra and was described by the UK press as "exceptional by any standards". Tom works from a studio in Oxfordshire where he lives with his wife Emily and their 2 daughters.

EDGE OF SOMETHING

Words and Music by Jamie Cullum
and Steve Booker

EVERYTHING YOU DIDN'T DO

Words and Music by
Jamie Cullum

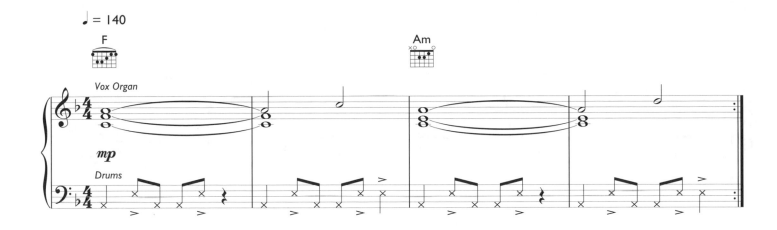

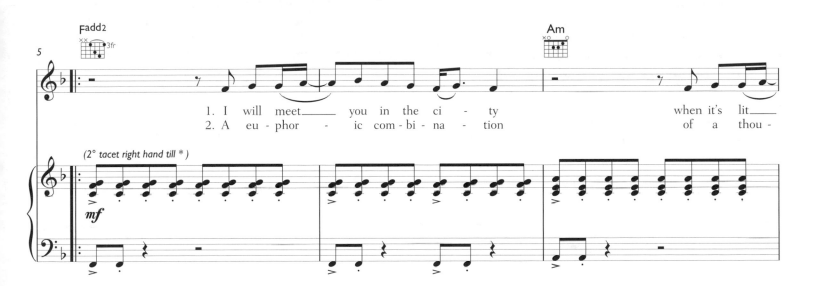

WHEN I GET FAMOUS

Words and Music by
Jamie Cullum

LOVE FOR $ALE

Words and Music by Cole Porter
and Rodney Hylton Smith

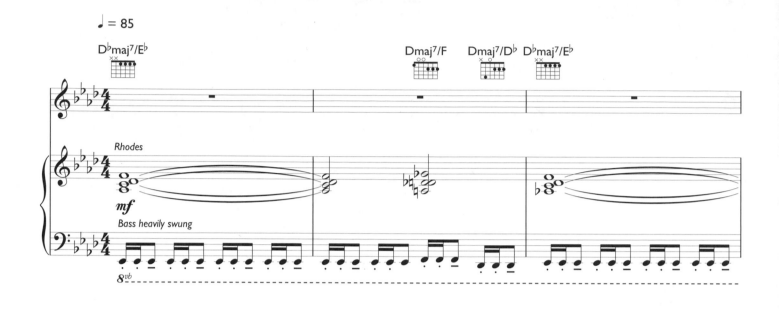

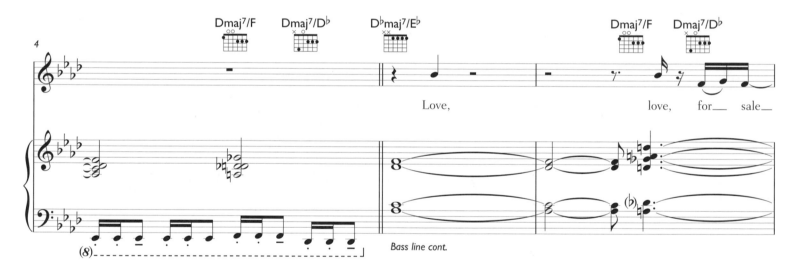

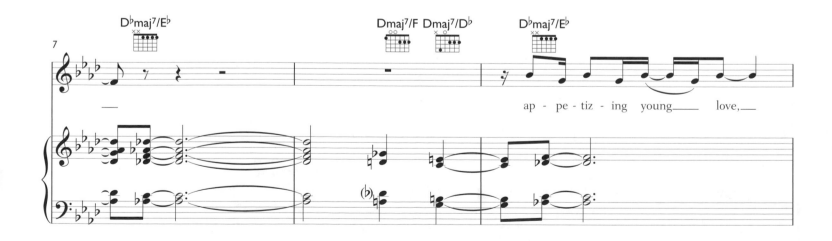

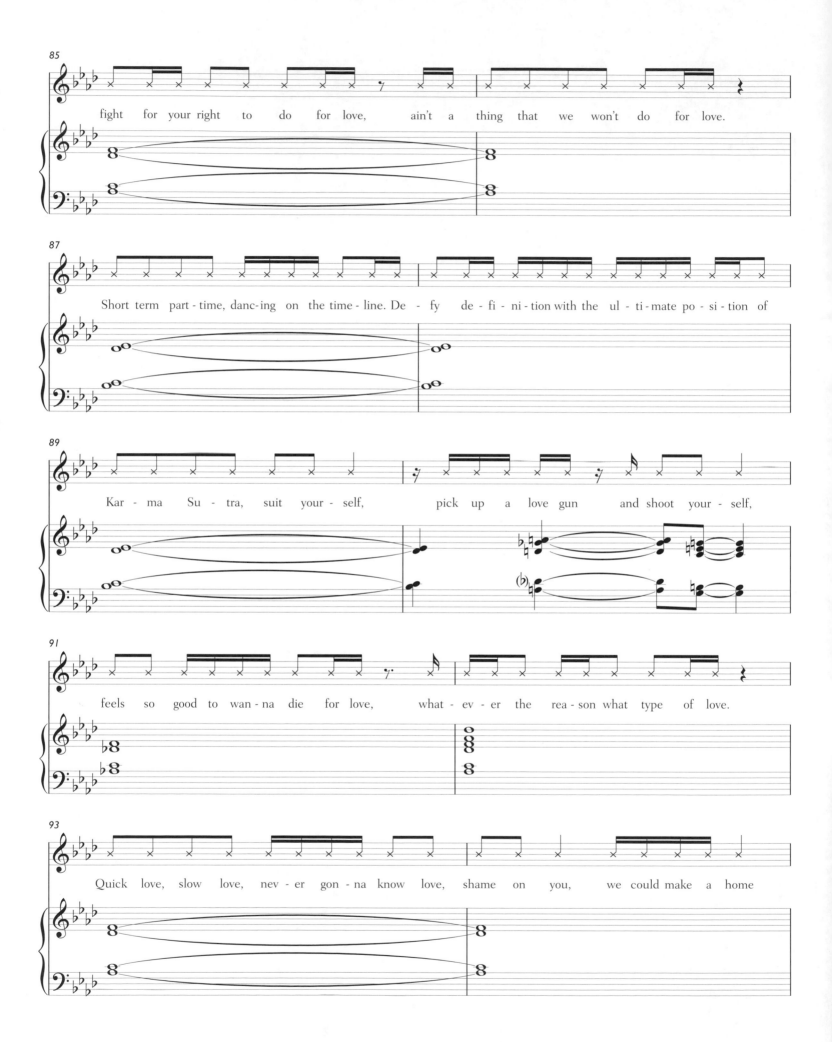

PURE IMAGINATION

Words and Music by Leslie Bricusse
and Anthony Newley

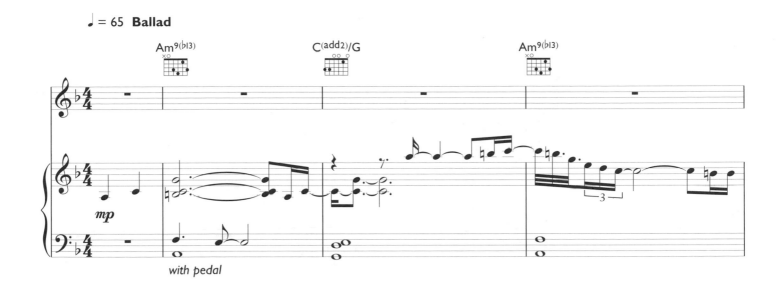

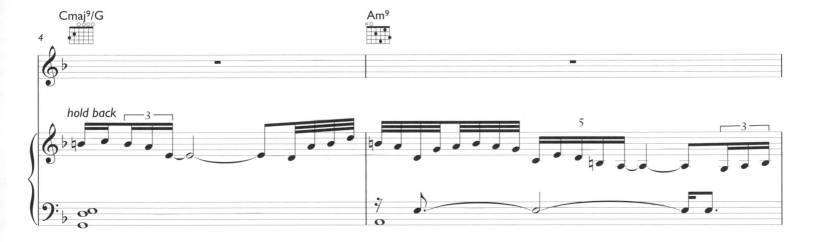

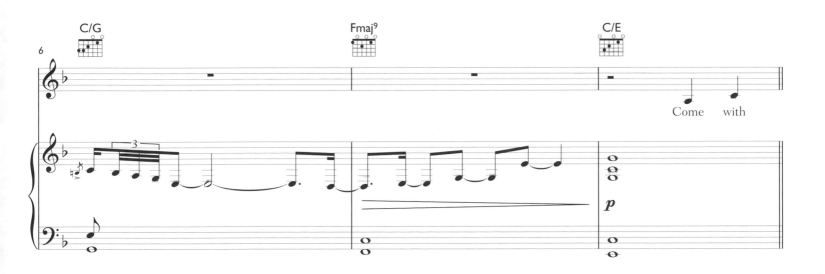

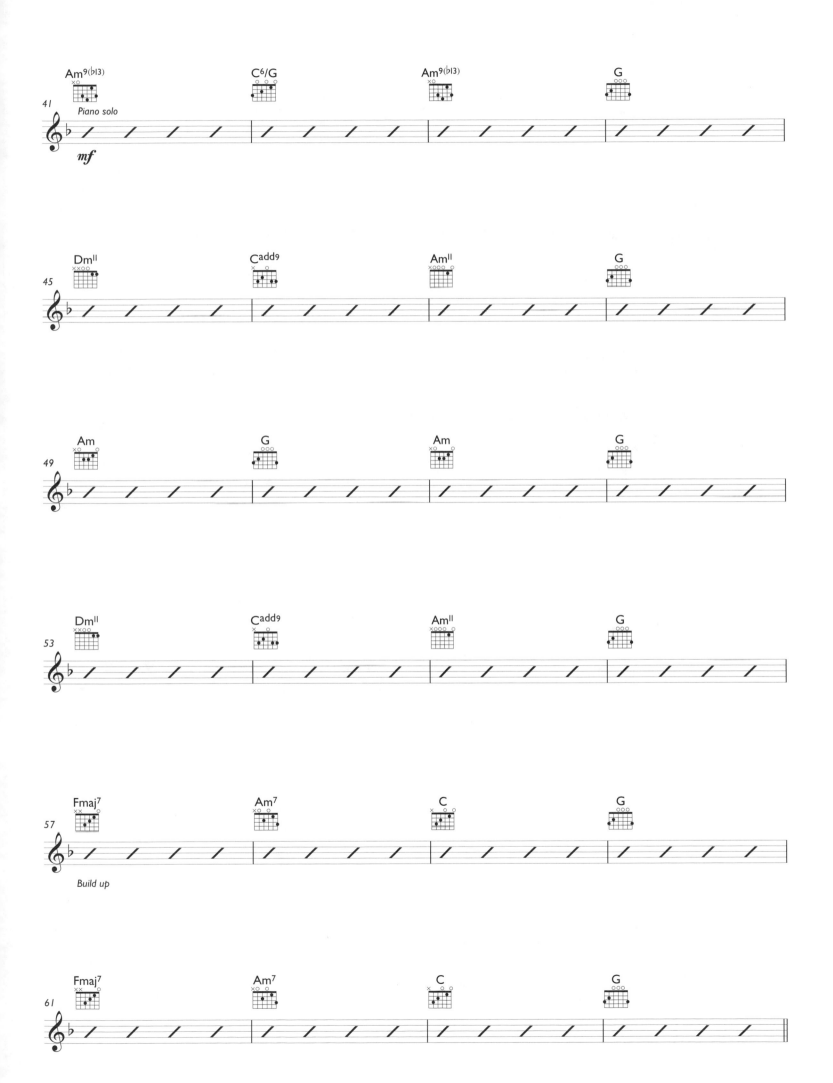

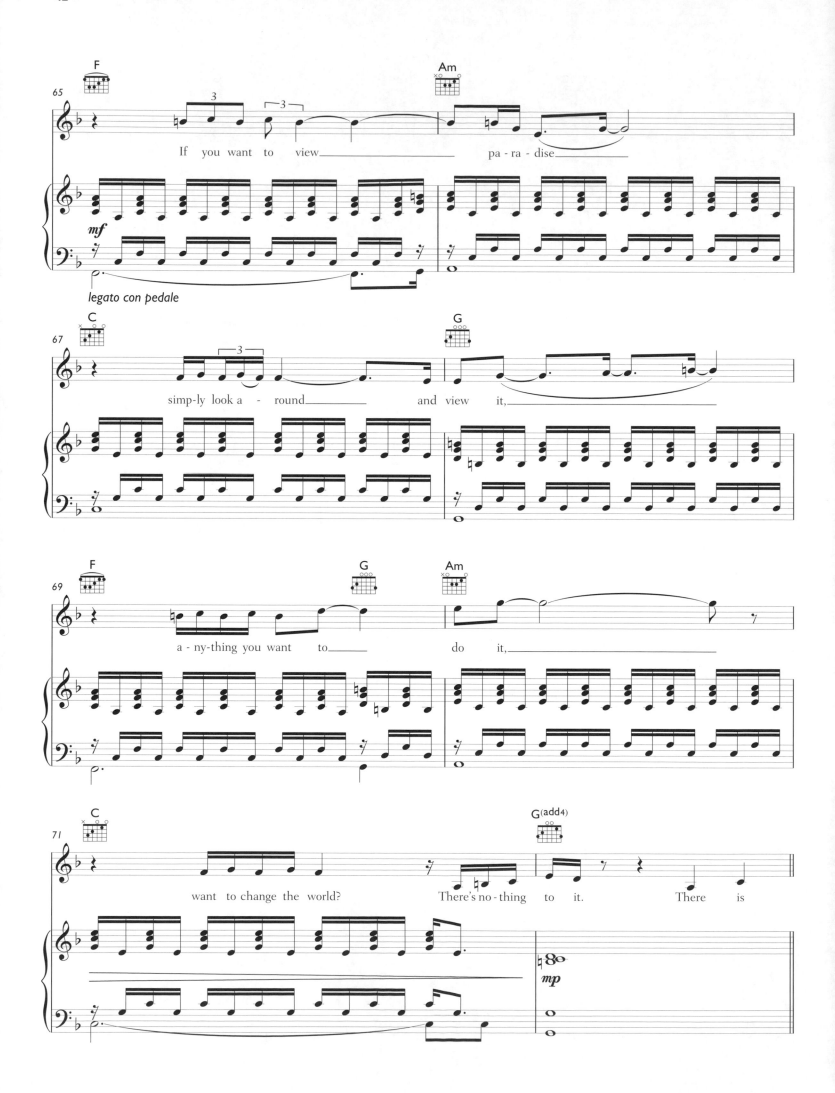

ANYWAY

Words and Music by Jamie Cullum,
Richard Poindexter, Robert Poindexter,
Jackie Members, Darren Lewis and Iyiola Babalola

1. Two bit phil-o-so-pher with point-less proc-la-ma-tions on his t - shirt,____
2. Al-ways re-mem-ber that the ter-ror-ists of time well, they ain't friend-ly,____

SAD SAD WORLD

Words and Music by
Jamie Cullum

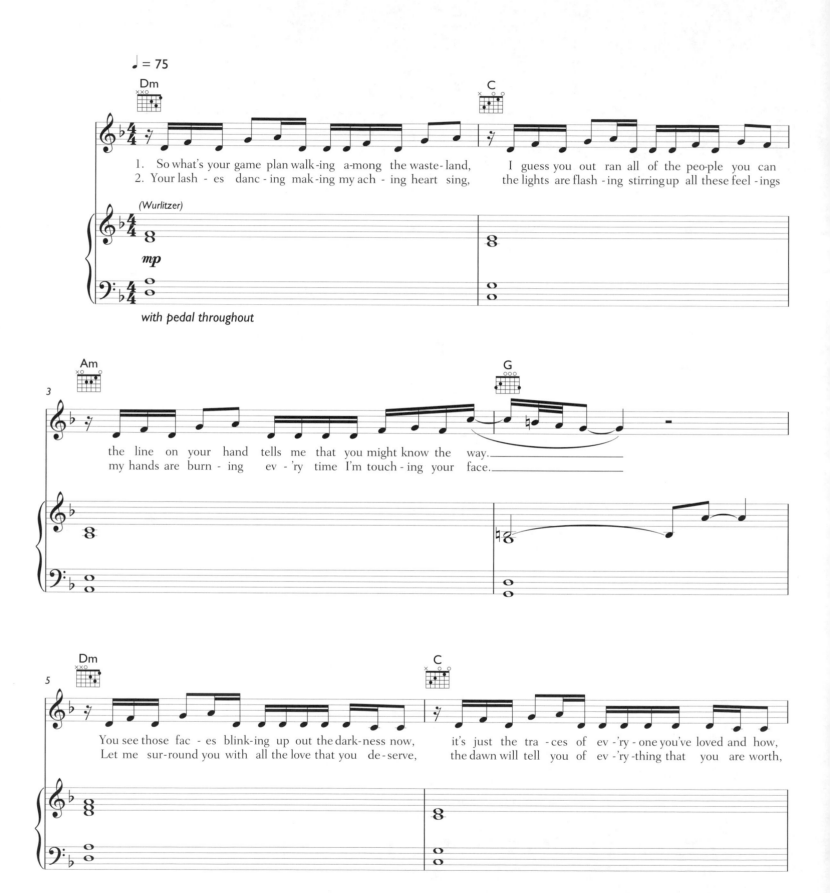

TAKE ME OUT

Words and Music by
Jamie Cullum

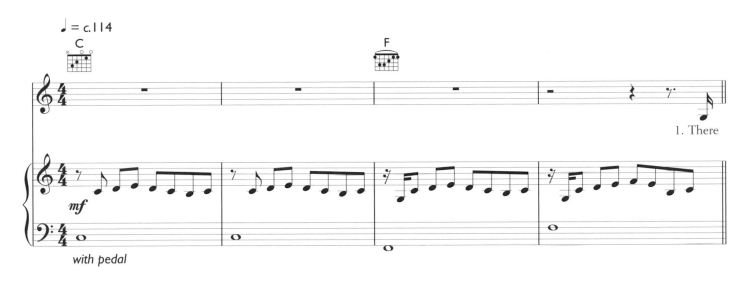

1. There

was an age___ the bat-tered time___ was coil-ed up___ a-round___ you like___ a dia-
(2.)crossed the line___ so ma-ny times___ it's noth-ing more than chalk___ wiped off___ a dark-

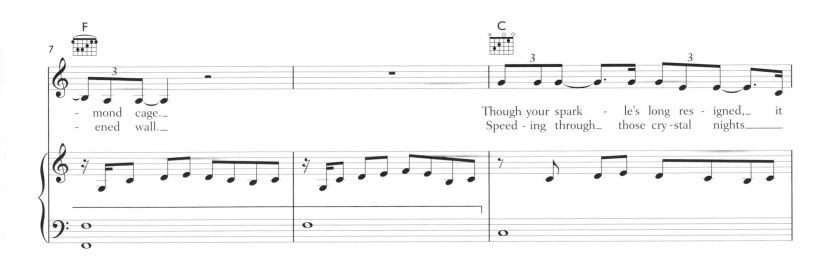

-mond cage.___   Though your spark - le's long res-igned,___ it
-ened wall.___   Speed-ing through___ those cry-stal nights___

SAVE YOUR SOUL

Words and Music by Jamie Cullum
and Ben Cullum

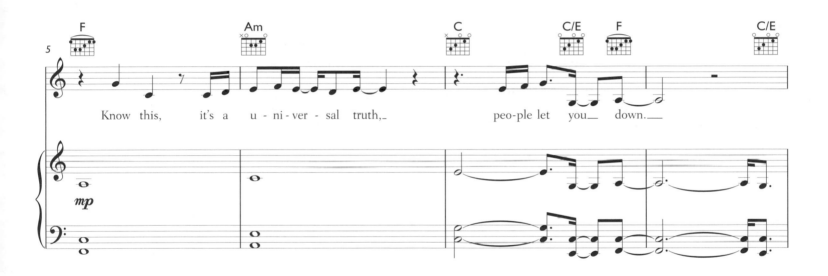

Know this, it's a u-ni-ver-sal truth,_ peo-ple let you_ down._

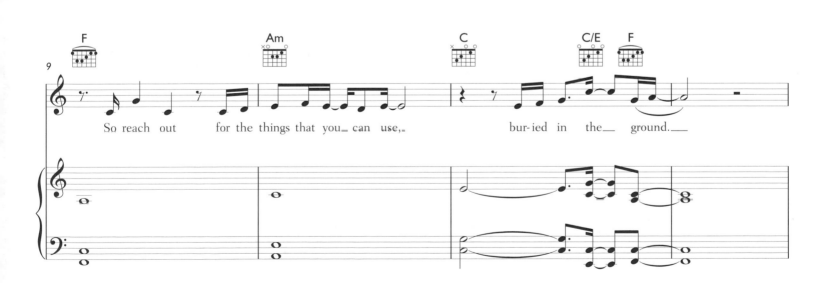

So reach out for the things that you_ can use,_ bur-ied in the_ ground._

GET A HOLD OF YOURSELF

Words and Music by
Jamie Cullum

Recorded on (4 string) tenor guitar tuned to C, G, D, A with capo on fret 3.
Chord symbols below are for standard guitar tuned to D, A, E, B (mute top 2 strings throughout).

Get a hold   of___your - self_____   now.___

YOU'RE NOT THE ONLY ONE

Words and Music by Jamie Cullum
and Ben Cullum

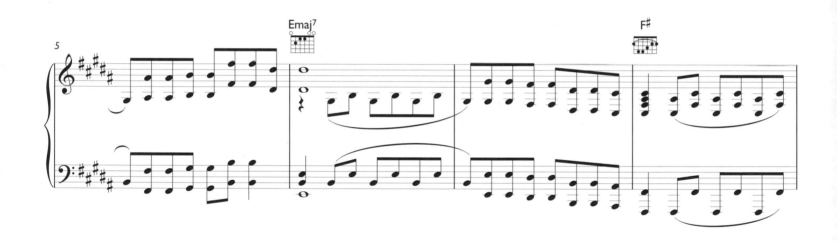

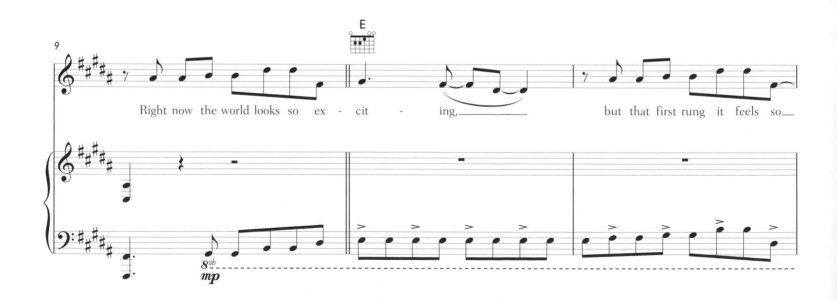

Right now the world looks so ex-cit - ing,_____ but that first rung it feels so_

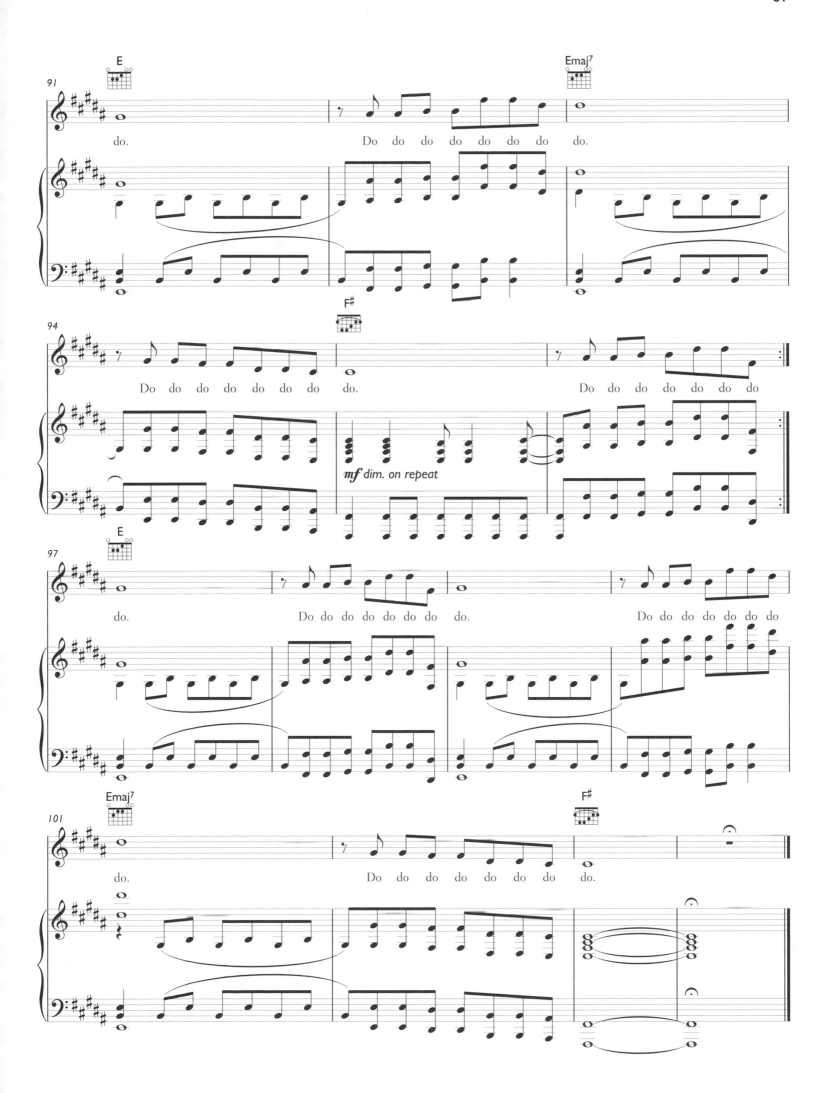

MOMENTUM

Words and Music by
Jamie Cullum

COMES LOVE

Words and Music by Lew Brown,
Charles Tobias and Sam Stept

Comes a rain-storm____ put your rub-bers on your feet, comes____
Comes a fire____ then you know just what to do, blow____

____ a snow-storm_ you can get a lit-tle heat.
____ a tyre____ you can get a-no-ther shoe.